Maui Ocean & Beach

IMAGES OF AN ISLAND

Photo editor

Douglas Peebles

Mutual Publishing

Maui

HONOLUA BAY
KAPALUA BAY
NĀPILI BAY
Honokōhau
Kapalua
Nāpili
KAHAKULOA BAY
HAKUHE'E POINT

Ho'okipa Beach — Maliko Gulch
Kanahā Beach Park
Pa'uwela
Jaws

Kā'anapali

Pu'u Kukui
Volcano
Wailuku
PA'IA BAY
Pā'ia
Ha'ikū
Pe'ahi

Ke'anae
Peninsula

Lahaina
Pu'unēnē
Kahului
Baldwin Park
Hāli'imaile
Makawao
Ke'anae
Arboretum
Wailua
Nāhiku

Hanakao'o
Beach Park
Olowalu
Mā'alaea
Pukalani
Pua'a Ka'a
State Park
Hāna
Highway
Pi'ilanihale Heiau
Wai'ānapanapa
State Park

MĀ'ALAEA BAY
Kīhei
Kula
Wai'ānapanapa
Hāna

Wailea Beach
Wailea
Polipoli Springs
Haleakalā National Park

Little Beach
Mākena
Kīpahulu

Molokini Islet
'Ulupalakua
Kaupō

Mākena (Big)
Beach

LA PÉROUSE BAY

Photo on pg. 3 © Douglas Peebles
All photos copyrighted by the individual
photographers noted in each caption.

ISBN-10: 1-56647-990-8
ISBN-13: 978-1-56647-990-5

First Printing, May 2013

Mutual Publishing, LLC
1215 Center Street, Suite 210
Honolulu, Hawai'i 96816
Ph: 808-732-1709 / Fax: 808-734-4094
Email: info@mutualpublishing.com
www.mutualpublishing.com

Printed in China

Introduction

To say Maui offers a little something for everyone is an understatement. The waters surrounding this Hawaiian island can be calm and relaxing in one location but adventurous and vicious just a short distance away. Whether your preference is seeing up-close the array of sea life and its vibrant colors beneath the crystal-clear waters by way of snorkeling, paddleboarding and kayaking, or if you're looking for more of a challenge with pursuits like kiteboarding and surfing, Maui offers whatever you desire.

From the white sand at the ever-popular Baldwin Beach on the North Shore to the lava-rock fields, reefs and other mysteries of La Pérouse Bay on its southern shores, you can experience something different each day of your visit. Kāʻanapali Beach in West Maui, once named America's Best Beach, also offers an abundance of options for water lovers.

What better place to learn the ins-and-outs of windsurfing than the very place it's been perfected? See the awe-inspiring waves where history was made by surfing legends like Laird Hamilton and Jeff Rowley, but if your goal is learning the basics, then stay away from the likes of Peʻahi and Hoʻokipa. Kite Beach, aptly named for its perfect kitesurfing conditions, is *the* place to go for lessons or just to watch more experienced kiteboarders put on a show. Bodyboarding and outrigger canoe paddling are as popular as other water sports – enjoy the topsy-turvy antics of one and learn about the rich Hawaiian history of the other.

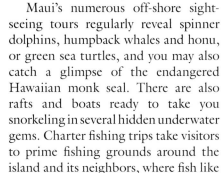

Maui's numerous off-shore sight-seeing tours regularly reveal spinner dolphins, humpback whales and honu, or green sea turtles, and you may also catch a glimpse of the endangered Hawaiian monk seal. There are also rafts and boats ready to take you snorkeling in several hidden underwater gems. Charter fishing trips take visitors to prime fishing grounds around the island and its neighbors, where fish like the mahimahi, marlin and the ever-popular ʻahi tuna will put up lengthy, feisty fights.

As always, safety comes first in unfamiliar waters, but there are memorable experiences awaiting all levels of water-sports enthusiasts, descriptions of what you'll encounter in and around Maui's surf, and plenty of other information in the following pages in order to make the most of your aloha experience.

Silhouettes like this one are an everyday occurrence on Maui's southern shores, which offer a great number of surfing spots throughout the year. Although the waves may not be as well known as those on the North Shore, there's no better place to learn the basics, better your skills or just enjoy some fun on the board. *Photo © David Olsen*

4

The Puʻu Ōlaʻi cinder cone probes the ocean off Mākena, with Little Beach on the western side and Big Beach stretching east. As long as the water isn't too rough or the current too strong, you can snorkel the reefs on the Little Beach side. If that doesn't work out, climb the rise between the two beaches and snap beautiful scenic photographs that are sure to be the envy of everyone back home. *Photo © Douglas Peebles*

Maui's waters are breathtaking from the air as they curve in and out around shorelines that include sandy beaches, mountains and those never-ending sugarcane fields. However, the fun really begins at sea level, where countless water sports and other activities await. Check the surf and weather reports and keep a flexible schedule in order to take advantage of all Maui has to offer. *Photo © Douglas Peebles*

Thread-like wakes trail windsurfers across the shallow, turquoise waters of Kanahā Beach Park. The Kahului Airport runway is visible at upper right. Kanahā Beach Park is a haven for water-sports enthusiasts of all skill levels and types, whether you prefer windsurfing and kiteboarding or surfing and canoe-paddling.
Photo © Douglas Peebles

Little has changed at Little Beach since it was part of a popular hippie colony in Mākena in the late 1960s. Located on Maui's southern coastline, Little Beach is tucked away behind a bluff that separates it from Big Beach, but unlike its neighbor, clothing remains optional. Nowadays, all types of people frequent the beach, which is as lovely and peaceful as any you'll find in the Islands, and you can even catch a drum circle and more entertainment on Sunday evenings as the sun goes down. *Photo © Darrell Wong*

Mākena's Oneloa (long sand) beach forms a mile-long crescent along Haleakalā's sunny southern shore. The steep sand bank at the water's edge is an indication that the tranquil-looking waves can quickly rise and crash into the beach, which is why this spot is popular with bodyboarders. *Photo © Douglas Peebles*

Kāʻanapali Beach's sun cabanas offer a view of the island of Lānaʻi. At the north end, referred to by locals as the Sheraton end (areas of the beach are usually referred to by the hotels along the sand), is Puʻu Kekaʻa (Black Rock), where a cliff diver performs each evening. Parallel and almost adjacent is Whalers Village, which features prime shopping venues, restaurants and more. *Photo © David Fleetham*

Framed by the West Maui Mountains, Kāʻanapali Beach radiates luxury and relaxation from its beautiful three miles of white sand and nearby two championship golf courses. Its waters are home to friendly sea turtles and a variety of brightly colored tropical fish, with great conditions for stand-up paddle boarding. There are even a few spots suited to surfing. *Photo © David Fleetham*

Hoʻokipa, located approximately two miles east of Pāʻia on Hāna Highway 380, is not for the faint of heart. Home to expert surfers and windsurfers alike, Hoʻokipa is rocky and treacherous at any time of year. Spectators can see the entire show from their vantage point at Hoʻokipa Lookout, but there's also a beach that's accessible to everyone. Surfers tend to prefer the eastside of Hoʻokipa, known as the "Pavilions." *Photo © Rex Tesoro*

Jet skis, helicopters, boats ... there's much more in the water than just surfers when the big waves arrive at Jaws. It takes teamwork to achieve a successful ride when the size of the waves prevent surfers from paddling in, and the extra help doesn't diminish the thrill in the least. *Photo © David E. Schoonover*

You're not just riding a wave at Honolua Bay; you're outrunning it. Surfers are dropped into the waves at speeds nearing 30 miles per hour. The best time to catch a glimpse of these monster waves is during the winter months, specifically November through March, but they don't happen daily, so always check the surf reports.
Photo © Quincy Dein

Laird Hamilton, shown taking on a colossal wave at Jaws, is one of the best-known surfers to conquer Pe'ahi. Hamilton was one of the first surfers to popularize the tow-in method, which allows surfers to catch bigger and faster waves they couldn't catch by paddling in. "Fearless" is the best way to describe this famous surf pro.
Photo © Darrell Wong

Ho'okipa is probably the most famous windsurfing spot in the world. Several contests are held here yearly. An interesting fact about Ho'okipa is that, like other beaches around Maui, windsurfers must wait until late morning to enter the water; however, unlike other surf spots, if 10 or more surfers are still in the break, the windsurfers have to wait. This is called Ho'okipa's "Ten Man Rule." *Photo © Douglas Peebles*

Windsurfing gear, like these pictured at Kanahā Beach, continue to become easier to use and more stable. If you're a beginner, schedule a lesson with any of several local kitesurfing companies and head to their training grounds at one of Maui's beaches. They will outfit you with the best gear for your body type and skill level in order to make the most out of your windsurfing experience. *Photo © Douglas Peebles*

Maui is the world capital of windsurfing and nowhere is more impressive, or dangerous, than the site known as Jaws. Windsurfers, like Robby Naish seen here, were the first to ride it. The sport has only grown in popularity, whether a person is interested in obtaining a "freeride" board used for more relaxed recreational use or a slalom board for high speeds. *Photo © Darrell Wong*

The Hoʻokipa Beach shoreline is commonly dotted with the bright colors of sails used by windsurfers and the beach gear of those more interested in watching them skim the waves. In the distance, fields of sugarcane lead the way to Maui's upcountry. *Photo © Douglas Peebles*

Awe-inspiring moves such as this one are just part of the thrill of kiteboarding, which, unlike its surfing counterpart, doesn't require waves to have a big day on the water. *Photo © Douglas Peebles*

Kite Beach, located at Kanahā Beach Park on Maui's northern shoreline and home to beginning and expert kiteboarders alike, has more windy days than any other location in the world, making it the ideal place to kiteboard or kitesurf, as it is also known. Kiteboarding combines the best features of several water sports but is widely recognized by its acrobatics, jumping and flying. *Photo © Quincy Dein*

Tandem kiteboarding can be used for instructional purposes but also just for fun, as seen here at Kanahā Beach Park, widely known as the birthplace of modern kitesurfing. Professionals from around the world travel to Maui to hone their skills, and variations of the sport are already in play, such as snow-kiteboarding.
Photo © Bob Bangerter

Canoe Beach (Hanakaōʻō Beach Park), the southern extension of Kāʻanapali Beach, got its name because it's the launching spot for outrigger canoes from Kahanā, Lahaina and Nāpili canoe clubs. It's also a good place to swim and paddleboard – go in the mornings for calmer surf or if you like a challenge, head out in the afternoon. Once on the water, make sure to take in the mesmerizing scenery of Maui's western shoreline. *Photo © David Fleetham*

Stand-up paddleboarding, especially in and around Mākena Beach Park, offers amazing views of the landscapes above the surface as well as the creatures and sea life below. Paddleboarders can see Big Beach and Little Beach on Maui's south side as well as Kahoʻolawe, the rim of Molokini and even Lānaʻi off in the distance. *Photo © Ron Dahlquist*

La Pérouse Bay, located by the Ahini-Kīna'u Natural Area Preserve, is an adventure in itself. Its rocky coastline presents caves and crevices, but snorkeling and paddleboarding are best when done in the morning hours – otherwise, it can get rough. Head south on Mākena Alanui Road past Big Beach and you'll find it at the very end. *Photo © Bob Bangerter*

Perhaps you want to strike out on the open water? Try a sport like kayaking at the very southern Lahaina end of Kāʻanapali Beach, where there's never a shortage of breathtaking views and an array of opportunities to see something you may not see anywhere else, like a whale breaching or a sea turtle's head bobbing just above the surface. *Photo © David Fleetham*

Kapalua Bay, located on Maui's northern west side, is a sheltered cove thanks to the outer reefs that help give it a C-shape. It's widely known for its snorkeling, but kayakers also enjoy its peaceful waters and beautiful scenery. *Photo © David Fleetham*

Olowalu Beach is long and narrow and features a shallow reef that is ideal for snorkeling, kayaking and even a little boogie boarding or beginning surfing. You'll get amazing views however you access the water, especially the further out you go where the reefs almost reach the surface of the water, forming columns.
Photo © Ron Dahlquist

Outrigger and sailing canoes representing the various districts of Maui come ashore at Wailea Beach on the south side of the island, where they are welcomed by ceremonial greeter Kimokea Kapahulehua. Outrigger canoes are as much a part of Hawai'i's culture today as they were long ago. *Photo © Shane Tegarden*

A men's team from Maui's Kīhei Canoe Club blasts up and over a whitecap during the annual Molokaʻi Hoʻe channel race, which is a 40-mile event that spans the Kaiwi Channel between Molokaʻi and Oʻahu. The race originated in 1952 and is held each fall, with men's and women's races held on separate weekends. Crews from all over Hawaiʻi and the Pacific compete each year. *Photo © Shane Tegarden*

On a practice or race day, Kīhei Canoe Harbor, home to Maui's Kīhei Canoe Club, is crowded and bustling with activity. But the views from the beach, especially towards the West Maui Mountains, are breathtaking no matter what time you're there. Visitors interested in canoe paddling can arrange to take part in an instructional paddling program offered by the club, which is available on Tuesdays and Thursdays as long as the weather cooperates. *Photo © Terrie Eliker*

Kāʻanapali Beach is the signature beach of West Maui with its three miles of pristine white sand and was formerly the vacation spot of Maui royalty. Now, the beach and its clear water provide a little something for everyone – canoe paddling, snorkeling, bodyboarding, surfing, catamaran sailing and more. Make sure to watch for cliff divers – Kāʻanapali's Puʻu Kekaʻa (or Black Rock, as it's commonly known) helped make the beach famous.
Photo © Rob DeCamp

The back side of Kahoʻolawe, a smaller island just off the southern coast of Maui, features a deeper water ideal for charter fishing trips. If your goal is to catch mahimahi, tuna, trevally, or one of a variety of marlin, as well as several other species of fish, schedule a 6- or 8-hour trip with one of Maui's charter-fishing tours.
Photo © David Fleetham

Yachts, fishing boats, dive tour craft and whale watching vessels in the afternoon sun line a section of the Lahaina Harbor. Whatever your fancy, you can find it here – Lahaina Harbor is one of the most popular spots on Maui to depart from for an offshore trip. *Photo © Douglas Peebles*

Crescent-shaped Molokini is an easily recognized feature off Maui's southern shoreline, but before it was mostly submerged, it looked very different as a cinder cone on Haleakalā. The protected marine wonderland provides endless delights for snorkelers who don't mind a short trip from one of Maui's harbors. *Photo © Douglas Peebles*

Mile Marker 14 at Olowalu is a longtime snorkeling stop for Maui visitors who appreciate the site's ease of access, abundant coral, and calm, clear viewing. If you must put your feet down, make sure to do so in a sandy area so as not to damage the reef or the bottoms of your feet. You may even see a few reef sharks casually swimming by.
Left photo © Ron Dahlquist; right photo © David Olsen

Raccoon butterflyfish are just one type of sea life you can find schooling over shallow Maui reefs. Spots like these are easily accessible from shore thanks to the island's numerous "put-in" locations, although deeper dives and more remote sites are also available for those wanting some variety. *Photo © David Fleetham*

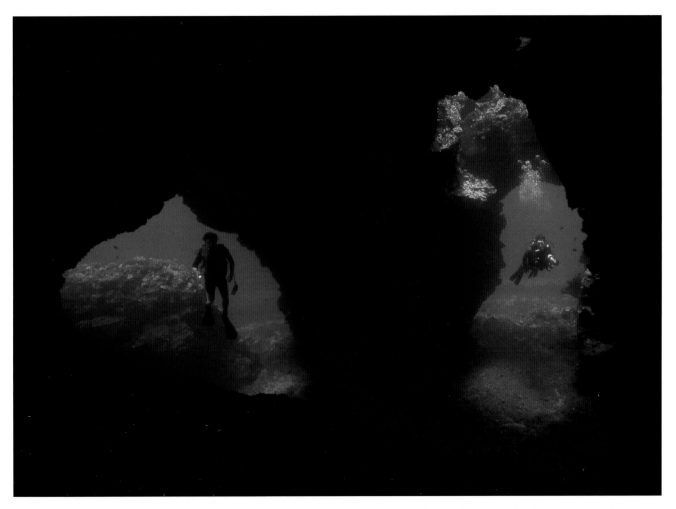

Lāna'i, one of Maui's neighbors, offers underwater cathedral cave foundations like these for divers. In several popular dive sites, visibility can sometimes reach 200 feet. Contact local dive companies to take you to the best dive spots in Maui County. *Photo © David Fleetham*

North Pacific humpback whales are a favorite sight in Maui's waters after they migrate from Alaska during the winter months. Although you can see the whales from several different vantage points around the island throughout the day, whale-watching tours offer a great deal of insight into the whales' mannerisms and habits, and will also likely get you a bit closer to the actual mammals themselves. *Photo © Scott Mead*

Few Maui sights are more dramatic than seeing a 40-ton humpback whale breach in open water. The splash from a good breach can be seen for miles. If you're visiting the island anytime from December to early May, make sure to schedule a whale-watching cruise for an opportunity to see the mammals up close. *Photo © Michael and Monica Sweet*

Hawaiian spinner dolphins are the acrobats of the waters around Maui. Whether they're leaping head-over-tail, spinning in the air, performing slaps with their heads and tails, or skimming alongside a boat, these playful ocean mammals always do their part in sharing the aloha spirit. The Hawaiian variety differs by shape and color.
Photo © David Fleetham

Hawaiian spinner dolphins get their name honestly from their above-water antics. Spinner dolphins have been known to spin up to seven times before splashing back into Maui's crystal-clear seas. There are many guesses as to why they spin, from courtship displays to simply being extremely happy and more, but whatever the case, spinner dolphins can be counted on to entertain. *Photo © Michael S. Nolan*

A diver grabs hold of a whale shark traveling through the waters off Kahoʻolawe. Whale sharks are common off the coast of Maui and its surrounding islands, and the gentle creatures which aren't really whales at all are easily recognized by their spots. Whale sharks have been documented to be as large as a bus and can weigh up to 37 tons. *Photo © Michael S. Nolan*

An akule baitball, a school of fish such as the one shown here, can be found off the shores of Maui and its size and organization is nothing short of impressive. Baitballs are comprised of thousands of the same type of fish, such as amberjacks and big eyed scad, and can measure 40 feet and larger in size. *Photo © Marty Wolff*

The Hawaiian green sea turtle (honu), is the most common type of turtle in Hawaiian waters. Adult honu can reach 200 pounds. They are primarily vegetarian, feeding on algae, seaweed and other plants around the coral reefs and rocks located in shallow water. Green sea turtles can live from 60 to 70 years and are a "threatened" species due to hunting, disease and loss of habitat. *Left photo © Harry L. Donenfeld, Right photo © David Fleetham*

Green sea turtles are a much-loved fascination in and around Maui's waters. They cruise the reefs and rarely seem bothered by anything, occasionally poking their heads above water for a few seconds before dipping below to continue on their way. Remember to admire them from a distance, however – honu are protected and their population is recovering from years of being hunted. *Photo © Michael S. Nolan*

Hawaiian monk seals, one of only two remaining monk seal species, spend nearly two-thirds of their time in the water surrounding the Islands. The official state mammal of Hawai'i enjoys hunting the fish, spiny lobsters, eels and octopuses found among the reefs, only heading to the beaches to rest or find shelter from storms. Hawaiian monk seals typically travel alone or in small groups, and their numbers are limited, so efforts are being made to ensure their survival. *Photos © David Fleetham*

The Maui Ocean Center, located on Wailuku's Māʻalaea Road, is just minutes away from the ocean its inhabitants come from, and mirrors perfectly the fish and sea life in Hawaiʻi's waters. It features numerous exhibits including a clear tunnel leading through a 750,000 gallon saltwater aquarium and the Tide Pool where invertebrates can be touched. All its sea creatures—green sea turtles, coral reefs, sharks and rays—are only taken from Hawaiian waters and only pumped in ocean water is used. *Photo © Al Hummel*

47

The easy-going surf town of Pā'ia on Maui's North Shore attracts a variety of people with its unique shops, eateries and beaches, as well as mesmerizing sunrises like this one. The waters off this North Shore spot can be calm one minute and a challenge the next for even the most advanced surfers. Dotting the shoreline are secluded little beaches and beach-front homes. *Photo © Harry L. Donenfeld*